Kimberly Lord

Animal Care

A Guide for The Animal Welfare Officer

Animal Welfare Consulting

Note for Librarians: A cataloguing record for this book is available from Library and Archives
Canada at www.collectionscanada.ca/amicus/index-e.html
ISBN 1-4120-9571-9

Creative Agency:
Pelican Studios Inc., West Vancouver, BC, Canada

Project Editor:
SoundsWrite Communications, North Vancouver, BC, Canada

Sharon All, a friend, who gracefully helped with the first two drafts.

Veterinary:
Coast Mountain Veterinary Services in Whistler and Pemberton, BC, Canada

Photography:
Kyla Brown Photography, Vancouver, BC, Canada

Animal Care Photos:
Dreamstime Stock Photos

Printed in Victoria, BC, Canada. Printed on paper with minimum 30% recycled fibre.
Trafford's print shop runs on "green energy" from solar, wind and other environmentally-friendly power sources.

Offices in Canada, USA, Ireland and UK

Book sales for North America and international:
Trafford Publishing, 6E–2333 Government St.,
Victoria, BC V8T 4P4 CANADA
phone 250 383 6864 (toll-free 1 888 232 4444)
fax 250 383 6804; email to orders@trafford.com
Book sales in Europe:
Trafford Publishing (UK) Limited, 9 Park End Street, 2nd Floor
Oxford, UK OX1 1HH UNITED KINGDOM
phone +44 (0)1865 722 113 (local rate 0845 230 9601)
facsimile +44 (0)1865 722 868; info.uk@trafford.com
Order online at:
trafford.com/06-1326

10 9 8 7 6 5 4 3 2

Table of Contents

Table of Contents

This guide, created to aid the Animal Welfare Officer, is dedicated to the many people who devote their lives to helping animals.

A special thank you to "Wink" and "Bear" for being such good friends and to all the animals that have touched my life over the past 15 years.

KIMBERLY LORD

Animal Welfare Consulting

❝ Mercy to **animals** means
mercy to **mankind.** **❞**

~ **Henry Bergh**
Founder of ASPCA

The Animal Welfare Officer

PROFESSIONALISM

An Animal Welfare Officer should always respond in a professional manner. When called to attend a property, you should greet individuals with courtesy, identify yourself as an Animal Welfare Officer, and explain the reason for your visit. After investigating a complaint, it is up to you to determine what form of action to take. Actions may include: making a recommendation, giving reasons for compliance, writing a warning or ticket, summarizing and monitoring a situation, if necessary.

The professional Animal Welfare Officer should:

- Be on time for all appointments.
- Wear a tidy uniform and drive a clean duty vehicle.
- Always start with a good demeanor. Be courteous and respectful.
- Start every contact as low key as possible and keep the dialogue open.
- Treat every case and person fairly and with objectivity.
- Be a good listener and paraphrase for accuracy. Wait to talk and try not to interrupt.
- Educate and encourage responsible pet ownership.
- Understand your authority, duties, and familiarize yourself with your equipment.
- Use common sense and exercise discretion in choosing the best course of action.
- Be prepared and comfortable with your own decisions.
- Always sharpen your skills and be safe.

OFFICER SAFETY

Safety is of paramount importance to the Animal Welfare Officer. When responding to a request for service, you should be relaxed but alert. You should be conscious of variables that could affect your safety, the safety of the animal that you're dealing with, and the safety to the public. Try not to become complacent when responding to requests for service. Treat every call individually. Prior to the capture of any animal, consider the type of animal, its condition, obvious dangers, location, and public safety.

An Animal Welfare Officer must know how to create a **"reactionary gap"[1]** and deal with **serious threats, aggressive behaviour, multiple subjects,** and **changing environments.**

A Reactionary Gap

A *reactionary gap* means having enough space in order to be able to react to a situation. While interviewing people, you should have a reactionary gap and an athletic stance, with your forearms resting on your duty belt. It is much easier to raise your arms from this position than from the sides. Animal Welfare Officers are trained to watch dog behavior, but it is just as important to be aware of an owner's body language. An owner will protect his or her animal like a child and will display warning signals, which could lead the owner to act out in a physical response. A reactionary gap also applies to catching and restraining animals safely. It is necessary to have a plan of action and quickly place a captured animal into a duty vehicle.

Serious Threats

If you perceive a serious threat from a dog, you should get back to a vehicle or another safe place. If necessary, you should use a door against the dog in order to get free or gain some distance to enter the vehicle. Climbing onto a hood or top of a vehicle is an option, but be prepared because dogs can climb too! If you are unable to get back to the vehicle without losing sight of the dog, stand motionless and have something out in front of you as a deterrent or offer to bite, such as a ticket book, bite stick, or a snare pole. Avoid direct eye contact by viewing the dog from your peripheral vision. If bitten, you should try to remain calm and not pull away. Many dogs will release their grip and stop biting. Fighting and pulling away will only increase the likeliness of a dog releasing its grip and biting again. In addition, you should watch out for silent dogs, which react aggressively when they are touched or when their collar is grasped. Try not to be fearful. DON'T ALLOW A DOG TO PULL YOU TO THE GROUND. If it happens, keep your arms firmly pressed against your neck and face.

Aggressive Behavior

Aggressive behavior may be demonstrated by a hard-to-deal-with person who is known by police. This could also include a person who has never had any dealings with authority and does not like a duty vehicle in their driveway or an Animal Welfare Officer knocking at their door. Aggressive behavior also applies to any dog or other animal with known aggressive responses. They must be handled safely and professionally from start to finish. Don't rush -- it only endangers safety.

Multiple Subjects

The term *multiple subjects* generally applies to multiple subject persons, but could easily include an owner and dog with known aggression. In this type of situation, disengage until backup is present, or attend with a second Animal Welfare Officer or the police. It is one thing to deal with a potentially dangerous dog, but it is another to deal with an owner who has a history of violence.

Changing Environments

As an officer, always be aware of your environment and surroundings. If executing a warrant (to seize a dog), is the owner being cooperative or uncooperative? Is there an object in the room that could be used by a desperate owner or a member of his family? Other factors to consider before attending are special knowledge about the history and previous dealings at the particular property. Is your environment safe? Remember to take care of yourself as the responder so you are able to help an animal or member of your community.

NOTE TAKING

It is imperative that an Animal Welfare Officer develop good habits early on in training for "complete, detailed and accurate notes."[2] For example: use black ink, draw lines through errors and initial them, and write complete notes (i.e. dates, times, phone calls, discussions, attending scene, etc.) at the time or soon after. In the event that you don't have a notebook, whatever you use to write on must be kept, and securely attached to an Officer File for safe record keeping.

"Many times an Animal Welfare Officer will not be able to make an Officer's File until after responding to several other calls or active cases."[3] It is important that you take the time to make detailed notes so that when you are later writing up the Occurrence Report, continuing with the investigation and testifying, you can accurately recall the details of the incident. Furthermore, notes can aid the prosecution if specific statements made by the subject, complainant or witness can be recalled. The most professional witness is one who can fully and accurately recall the events to the judge.

Detailed information must be obtained from all involved parties, including complete names, addresses, phone numbers, and a record of what the individual stated.

If there are multiple witnesses, rather than having all witnesses explain what has taken place, it is better to have one primary witness relay the incident as they saw it, and then gather the other witnesses' statements at a later time.

Be sure to separate witnesses when taking their statements so that their recollection of the event is in their own words, and not influenced by the other witnesses. If a person is reluctant to talk when others are present, they should be asked to provide a written statement. There may be times when an Animal Welfare Officer will want to interview the parties in person as this may help in determining the credibility of the statement. Being polite, remaining objective, and explaining the necessity for exact words and quotes will help the investigation.

The accuracy of the statement depends on the Animal Welfare Officer having written down exact quotes. It is not acceptable to simply paraphrase. The exact words, including obscenities and improper grammar, should be reflected in the quote. Do not go through your report and edit or interpret what you think they may have meant. If you have any questions or need clarification, your investigation is not complete.

Statements need to be signed and dated. This includes any statements that are provided to another agency or are part of an ongoing case in your department. This should also be done if you provide a photocopy of your notes to co-workers.

The use of diagrams can be helpful in remembering the details of a situation. In the field, the diagram will be small in your notebook, but can be drawn to a larger scale upon returning to the office. Any loose paper should be securely attached to the Officer File for safe record keeping.

Pictures should be placed in protective sheets and labeled with the date, time, location, and an explanation of the picture.

Example of a notebook entry:

> *Thursday, December 01, 2005*
> *Shift 09:00 - 17:00 hr.*
> *Work with [partners or coworkers names]*
> *High overcast -- raining lightly*

09:00 *On shift at shelter -- Assigned a new biting incident.*
09:12 *File 2005-4315*
Contacted Cst. BROWN at detachment regarding biting incident that occurred in the a.m. BROWN requested assistance to seize dogs involved in serious biting incident. One dog is still at large at location.

09:35 *Arrived on scene, met with Cst. BROWN, and was briefed of other details. One dog described as mixed breed, primarily black in color with spotted white markings, is still running loose around the neighborhood. Witness that came over to our vehicles from 4825 Huckleberry, said she saw one of the dogs go into her neighbor's backyard.*

09:40 *Attended to the neighbor's property pointed out by witness, and was able to approach a dog matching description. Dog was secured and then placed securely in vehicle without incident.*

At the end of the notes, draw a horizontal line across the page from left to right, then a diagonal line from right to left to the opposite bottom corner, and then a horizontal line across the bottom. The page should be finished with the signature of the Animal Welfare Officer.

Notes are a complete record of the events using the "Five W's Principle."

WHO -- Who witnessed an offense? Who was injured? Who was the attending veterinarian? Who are the reported attacking dogs?

WHAT -- What's the nature of the complaint? What happened? What was the degree of injuries? What was said by whom? What did your investigation determine?

WHERE -- Where did the incident occur? Where did you attend first? Where was the hospital or veterinarian clinic?

WHEN -- When was the call reported? When was the call dispatched? When did you arrive on scene? When did you update your complainants? When did you follow up?

WHY -- Why did this happen?

DUTIES OF THE ANIMAL WELFARE OFFICER

- Follow up a complaint with objectivity.
- Determine whether an offense has been committed.
- Act as a liaison with other agencies when something is reported and is determined to be outside of your jurisdiction or authority.
- Gather complete and accurate facts to help determine the outcome of the case.
- Record information in a chronological, clear, manner.
- Be able to prove all the elements of the offense and prove a history of non-compliance, if applicable.
- Be comfortable with your actions and determine the best course of action.
- Provide testimony that clearly and completely describes all of your actions to the Judge.

TESTIMONY TIPS

When testifying, the Animal Welfare Officer must present details of a case from memory, without reference to written notes.

The Animal Welfare Officer should:

- Recall events to the best of his or her ability by reviewing all notes prior to testifying.
- Arrive early and wait until called to testify.
- Never discuss the case.
- Have his or her notebook on hand.
- Bow to the judge upon entering the courtroom and walking to the witness box. The Animal Welfare Officer should expect to be prompted to give an oath, swear on the Bible, give his or her full name, etc.
- Remain calm and give the complete account of events in chronological order and all essential elements of the offense.
- Speak slowly, clearly, and without hesitation, allowing the judge to make notes. Use approximates for times, weights, etc. Show exhibits while describing them to the Judge.
- Give evidence that is both favorable and unfavorable, if applicable.
- Properly identify the accused (look towards and point out the accused, i.e. "Yes, your honour, that is Mr. Brown") when prompted.
- Ask permission to refer to notes when unable to recall information from memory, by addressing the judge as "Your honour" in Provincial court.
- Never assume that the judge will give permission. Instead, wait for an indication from the judge.
- Stop speaking if and when counsel objects.
- Produce your notes upon request. It is a good idea to mark the relevant sections using rubber bands or clips.

- Step down from the witness box and proceed to exit after all evidence has been given and cross-examination has been completed. Bow to the judge before you exit the court. The Animal Welfare Officer must be officially excused to leave the courthouse, as they may still be called back by the judge.

OFFICER AND ANIMAL FILE PRESENTATION

Animal Shelter Representatives are required to note messages and record incidents in an Occurrence Log and/or computerized record keeping program.

Some incidents are routine and are considered paperless files, which are opened and closed. An Officer's file jacket can be opened for incidents that have minimum to considerable documentation, and should be reviewed by a Senior Officer.

An Animal File can be opened when an animal is taken into a shelter. The Officer's file must have the same corresponding file number as the animal's file in the Occurence Log.

Officer File Presentation

- The Occurrence Report or "original complaint" shall be secured to the right hand side of an opened file.

- The left hand side of the opened file jacket may include: complainants and additional statements, questions and answers asked by the Animal Welfare Officer involving relevant information from conversations, veterinarian reports, pictures, diagrams, warning notices, letters, officer copy of any issued tickets, warrants, information reports, and a copy of your municipal bylaws and/or provincial statutory regulations.[4]

To summarize: attach the Occurrence Report to the right side and all other information to the left hand side of an open file jacket.

Animal File Presentation

When Shelter Representatives receive an animal and take it into a shelter -- strayed, surrendered, impounded, injured, or dead -- it must be noted in the "Occurrence Log" and/or into a computerized record-keeping program. It is important to have a hard copy of the documentation, and for your veterinarian to make notes.

- Attach an animal medical sheet to the front cover of a file jacket for note-taking by your attending veterinarian.

- The right hand side of an opened file jacket shall include a receiving animal printout sheet which lists: breed, sex, color, identification, owner notification, applicable fees, and condition of animal. Also, it may include any of the following shelter forms: surrender by owner, stray form, claimed by owner form, adoption waiver, evaluation, behavioral assessment, additional known medical health sheets (provided by former owner), passport information for new adoptive owner, foster form, plus any other related information pertaining to the animal.

- The left hand side of an opened file jacket shall include a blank sheet for shelter notes in chronological order, followed by their supporting documentation, e.g., Kennel Attendant's information, feedback from volunteer dog walkers, applications for adoption, adoption committee remarks (home check), and successful adoption information.

❝ A true cat lover
cradles a new kitten
and knows that **nine lives ❞**
will never be nearly enough
~ **Anonymous**

Dogs

COMMUNICATIONS

It is important that Animal Welfare Officers and Shelter Representatives develop keen observation skills to better understand and handle dogs in the field and in the shelter. You should pay attention to a dog's entire body and watch its body language. Make note of any changes that occur.

Ears

Relaxed: Neutral position, ears are standing up but relaxed

Frightened/Threatened: Back position, ears pulled back, down, and sometimes flat against head

Alert/Threatening: Up and forward position, ears appear closer together, skin on forehead wrinkles

Eyes and Gaze

Relaxed: Casual gaze

Distracted: Scans environment casually

Fear, Submission: Avoids eye contact (turns away or looks at ground)

Nervous, Fearful, Anxious: Scans environment frantically (eyes dart rapidly around)

Frightened: Dog may be too scared to look away

Threatened: Direct stare (rarely looks away)

Eyes

Not Aroused, Relaxed: Constricted pupils (small)

Frightened: Widened, lots of white showing

Fear, High Arousal: Dilated pupils (big)

Threatening: Squinting, partially shut

Mouth

Relaxed, Content: Mouth open, tongue partially out, skin around eyes relaxed (happy face)

Panting: Dog is too warm or can indicate stress

Lower Arousal Level: Closed mouth

Submission: Showing teeth but eyes somewhat closed, some will lick lips, submissive body postures (submissive grin)

Defensive Threat: Mouth opened wide, lips retracted horizontally to show more teeth

Offensive Threat: Mouth opened slightly, upper lip wrinkled vertically to show front teeth

Tail

Friendly Intent: Furious wagging

Fearful or Defensive: Lower tail carriage

Threatening: Slow, methodical, back-and-forth waving

Alert and Focused or Offensively Threatening: Held high and perfectly motionless

In general, the higher the tail carriage, the more alert or offensively motivated the dog.

Vocalizations

Submission or Excitement: High pitched barks

Warning: Low pitched barks

Submission, Wants Something, Pain: Whining

Threat: Growling

Separated from pack and is calling other members: Howling

Relaxed Dog

- Calm
- Body is soft
- Moves without tenseness or inhibition
- Weight is evenly distributed on all four feet (not leaning forward or leaning back)

Fearful/Defensive Dog

- Ears back
- Tail tucked
- Teeth showing - front and sides, if displayed
- Crouched or cowering
- Will not stand tall
- Head and neck held low
- Often sits down
- Will turn away from you
- May roll over and spread legs to expose belly

Invitation to play, behavior which follows should not be taken seriously: Bowing down (play bow)

Fearful and offensive dogs typically show forms of aggression by growling, snapping, lunging, or biting

Alert/Offensive Dog

- Muscles are tense
- Movements are less frequent and less fluid
- Head is held high
- Hackles may be raised on back
- More of dog's weight is carried on the front feet (as if ready to charge)
- Exaggerated approach behaviors including staring or visually tracking a victim

DO

- Talk calmly and use your friendly voice
- Turn side of body to dog
- Avoid eye contact and view the dog from your peripheral vision

- Crouch down, partially bend the knee, or stand straight up
- Keep hands at side
- Allow the dog to come to see and sniff you
- Watch for more than one dog and silent dogs displaying subtle body language

DON'T

- Directly face (square) to the dog
- Stare directly into eyes
- Lean over them
- Move quickly or suddenly towards the dog
- Allow the dog to circle behind you
- Allow a dog to pull you to the ground[5]

CATCH AND RESTRAINT

When you receive a call you need to ask yourself:

- **What kind of animal is it?**
- **Is it a biter?**
- **What should we use first?** Unless there is a known threat, use voice, leash, bait, and a "snappy snare". The safest place to approach is from the side and not directly from the front. If it is a dog, give a command of "sit", "want to go for a car ride?", or some other phrase the dog may recognize.
- **Is it sick or injured?** Is the animal unconscious or needing medical treatment?
- **Is it a traffic problem?** Think Officer safety first. Be aware of what is going on around you so you are able to safely assist.
- **Is there more than one animal?**
- **Where is it?**
- **Do you need help?**

Prior to any capture, consider the following points:

- Is the capture of the animal justified?
- What type of animal are you dealing with?
- What type of terrain are you on (i.e. slippery, rocky, sloped, etc.)
- Is the animal contained or able to escape?
- How is the condition and emotional state of the animal?

Dogs

Dogs can often be lured with food, leashed, and lifted into the duty vehicle. When lifting, place one hand under the dog's collar or leash, and with your free hand, assist the dog if needed. Watch and feel for sudden changes in behavior. If a dog turns its head quickly, push it away safely.

It is important to develop your skills to be ready for any aggressive response from a dog and to minimize risk to personal safety. If attending to a call or incident, have something in your hand (i.e. ticket book) that can, if needed, be placed between you and the dog should it attempt to bite. Give the dog a firm "Off" command and humanely utilize your equipment as necessary.

A snare pole should be in your hands when responding to true vicious or dangerous dog calls. If a vicious or dangerous dog is impounded, ensure other staff are informed. Do not handle the dog, especially after it has bitten, until it has had a chance to calm down, otherwise known as a "cool down period".

A dog that is injured should be restrained and muzzled before being lifted and transported. Any dog that is injured or sick should be given prompt medical treatment.

STRAYS

The following information should be noted when a stray dog is brought into a shelter:

Age

Dogs can be categorized into the following groups: puppy (under 12 months of age), young adult, mature adult (generally 2-8 years), senior, and geriatric.

Gender

To determine the dog's gender, look under the belly for genitalia and look for testicles.

Breeds and Descriptions

Animal Welfare Officers and Shelter Representatives should take the time to develop their knowledge of purebred dogs. The ability to accurately identify which type of breed or crossbreed you are dealing with is imperative when helping to return a stray dog to its rightful owner. A dog's markings should be accurately described and a potential owner should also be encouraged to visit the shelter to view the dog.

Identification

If the dog is wearing a collar, check to see if it has a license or a name tag with a phone number. Also, search the right ear and the inside of the rear thigh and groin area for any identifying tattoos. If an identification tattoo exists on an otherwise unmarked dog, the owner can be traced through a veterinarian facility or a local kennel club.

Animal shelters and most veterinarian facilities have microchip scanners. The scanner is used to scan an animal's shoulder area including the front of the shoulders and all surrounding areas in case a microchip has slipped. If a microchip is present, it can then be traced to the registered owner.

Condition

The condition of a dog should always be considered and noted. Most dogs that come into a shelter will be in "normal" condition, while others may be found to be in poor condition. This can vary from a dog being undernourished to obese, having a pre-existing medical condition that is being treated or in some cases not being treated, or a dog that has been injured while at large (i.e., hit by a car).

The "Medical Considerations" section is intended to aid in the evaluation of an animal brought into a shelter. It is meant to help the Kennel Attendant or the Animal Welfare Officer during straightforward evaluations and is not intended as a replacement for proper medical treatment.

A dog that does not warrant immediate medical treatment should be scheduled and checked by a veterinarian, if not claimed. If any doubt exists about the condition of the dog, a local veterinarian should be called or the animal should be transferred to be examined and to receive medical treatment, if necessary. Failure to do so could result in potential liability should an animal's condition degenerate while under care. If treated, the owner should be notified of any veterinary findings. Methods of cost recovery should be discussed with management.

Cats

COMMUNICATION

Cats communicate with all parts of their body and it is important to pay close attention to their movements as their behavior can change quickly. Use restraint techniques and safety equipment when necessary to prevent scratches and bites.

Whiskers

Content: Sticking straight out to the side

Afraid and Defensive: Flat against the cat's cheeks

Ears

Unsure, Considering Options: Ears back, steady posture

Defensive or Angry: Ears back, low body

Interested, Alert: Pricked ears

Eyes

Casual: Relaxed with normal sized pupil

Relaxation: Steady with several long, blinks

Annoyed: Narrow, dilated pupils

Fear, Threat: Direct stare, dilated pupils (big)

Mouth

Threat: Open, hissing, showing teeth

Tail

Annoyed: Entire tail moves back and forth

Severely Agitated, Threatening: Rapidly back and forth from the base

Conflict: Fully bristled, straight into the air (body sideways to appear larger)

Submissive, Afraid: "Puffed up" or bristled, cat may lower its tail or tuck it between its legs

Friendly, Excited: Raised tail, fur isn't bristled

Vocalizations

"Hello": Soft spoken "meow"

Demand for food or attention: Loud and drawn out "meow"

A cat is beckoning you: Soft "R" noise that ends in a trill

A cat is happy, or sometimes expressing extreme emotion (happiness, irritation or pain): Purring

Aggressive or Defensive Intentions: Hissing

Entire body language

Friendly, behavior content: Relaxed body, purring, meowing, arches back, curls its tail upward loosely and puts its head down, then rubs up against you

After something "stalking": Body is low, crawling

Submission and Readiness: Body shrinks, legs tucked underneath

Confidence and Aggression: Body expands, legs are extended, fluffing up

Fearful/Defensive Threat

A defensive, threatening cat will usually show one or more of the following body language:

- Standing up, back arched, tail straight up like a "Halloween cat"
- Ears are flat back against head
- Growls or hisses
- Turns side of body to another cat as defensiveness increases
- Wraps tail around its body while facing another cat

Alert/Offensive Threat

- Standing, rear hips higher than front and its tail is down
- Direct eye contact or staring
- Ears out to the side of head
- Growls and hisses

CATCH AND RESTRAINT

When working with cats, watch for warning signs that the cat may soon become aggressive. Aggressive behavior is generally direct-ed towards a person when the cat does not like the way it is being handled. To prevent scratches and bites, cats should be picked up using a firm grip to the scruff of the neck as this somewhat paralyzes them, reverting them back to when their mothers picked them up as kittens. With an extremely agitated cat, it may also be useful to tuck in and support hind legs or use a towel to wrap the cat up so it cannot move its arms and legs. The "cat tongs" may also be an effective tool when dealing with uncooperative or vicious cats. The contained cat should be placed in a transport cage for transferring and safekeeping.

Injured cats typically act aggressively as their instinct is to nurse their injuries on their own, and they may see you as a threat. In this case, they should be approached with protective gear and caution, and be restrained before any medical attention is given. Any cat that is injured or sick should be given prompt medical treatment. If an Officer is bitten, they should seek medical treatment, as cat bites are highly infectious.

Non-feral cats with serious forms of aggression should be examined to rule out any medical problems that may be the culprit of the aggressive behavior. If the cat is found to be medically sound, the use of a Certified Animal Behaviorist may be necessary.

STRAYS

The following information should be noted when a cat is brought into a shelter:

Age

A veterinarian can give an educated guess by looking at the cat's teeth and eyes. This information should be included in the animal's file. The veterinarian can age them into the following groups: kitten, young adult, senior and geriatric.

Gender

The gender of kittens and neutered cats can be determined by looking at the shape and proximity of the anus and the genitals. In females, the openings are close together. In males, the openings are further apart. Often, in very young male kittens, the testicles have not had a chance to drop, so it may be very hard to determine the gender at this point. The presence of testicles will indicate that the cat is an intact male.

Kitten: Immature cat
Queen: Intact female
Tom: Intact male

Breeds and Descriptions

Animal Welfare Officers and Shelter Representatives must take the time to develop their knowledge of purebred cats. The ability to accurately and clearly describe a cat is paramount in returning a stray cat to its rightful owner.

Condition

The condition of a cat coming into a shelter may vary, and should be taken under consideration and noted in the animal's file.

The "Medical Considerations" section of this guide is intended to aid in the evaluation of an animal brought into a shelter. It is meant to help the Kennel Attendant or the Animal Welfare Officer during straightforward evaluations and is not intended as a replacement for proper medical treatment.

A cat that does not warrant immediate medical treatment should be scheduled for examination by the attending veterinarian if not claimed. If any doubt exists about its condition, it should be transferred to a veterinarian facility as soon as possible. Failure to do so could result in potential liability should an animal's condition degenerate while under care. If the cat is treated, the owner should be notified of any veterinarian findings. Methods of cost recovery should be discussed with management.

Identification

Check the right ear for any identifying tattoos. If an identification tattoo exists in an otherwise unmarked cat, the tattoo can be traced through a veterinarian facility.

Animal shelters and most veterinarian facilities have microchip scanners. If a microchip is present, it can be traced to the registered owner.

Shelter Animals

SURRENDERED

Various animals fall under the category of *surrendered animal* such as animals turned over by an owner for adoption or strays turned in by a citizen.

Surrender By Owner

In the event any animal is surrendered, a surrendered animal form should be completed and all medical records must be provided. An owner surrender may also include a surrender fee governed under municipal bylaw or by donation to help pay for the future care of the animal until a life long home can be found. The form addresses transfer of ownership to prevent any future liability issues. An owner surrendering an animal must clearly understand that the animal will be placed in a new home or potentially euthanized, under certain circumstances.

Stray Animals

If an animal is brought in as a stray, Shelter Representatives must exhaust all efforts to notify an owner, i.e., identification tag, license, tattoo, and microchip. A stray must be held for a period specified under municipal bylaw. Municipal bylaw regulations provide that after holding an animal for a period of ninety-six hours it can be available for adoption. It is proposed that an animal be held for a full seven-day period. Experience has shown that some animals are claimed during or shortly after the ninety-six hour period due to extraordinary circumstances.

All animals at the shelter must be housed separately until the claiming period has expired, pending a veterinarian examination and vaccines, and behavioral assessment, if applicable. Kennels, cages, rooms, and playpen areas must first be sanitized with sanitizing solution for disease prevention. Information for each animal housed must be displayed on identification cards and/or whiteboards. This information should include: identification (ID tag, license, tattoo, microchip), temporary name, breed, color, age, sex, date of admission, and any necessary medical or behavioral warnings.

It is recommended that dogs wear a Martingale collar with tag, so they cannot slip out of the collar when walked by a volunteer dog walker. A white board should be implemented to clearly identify which dog can go out for walks with volunteers and the experience needed by its handler. Volunteers should attend a mandatory training session to be taught safe dog handling skills and techniques.

Cats can be collared and placed in a community cat room after the claim period, provided they've been given a clean bill of health by a veterinarian, vaccinated, and have been altered.

All animals must receive proper care and handling. This includes fresh water and food, a sanitized living area, opportunity for socialization, play and exercise, training (canines), bathing and grooming as needed, quality nutrition, administration of medication as directed by a veterinarian, and a secured environment. Efforts should be undertaken throughout the day to ensure animal waste is removed in a timely manner.

CLAIMED

In the event an animal is claimed, a claimed animal form should be completed and signed in keeping with policies and procedures. A person claiming an animal must provide proper identification, attest to ownership or be the person in care. Adopting this procedure provides protection from potential civil action should ownership of an animal be challenged by a third party.

HOMELESS (UNCLAIMED)

Any animal that is homeless should be examined by a veterinarian to determine the status of its health, if treatment is necessary, and that it is vaccinated and altered prior to the animal being adopted. If an animal is too young to be altered, the adoption agreement must require the new owner to have their animal altered by a date advised by a veterinarian to help control the animal population. Major illnesses should be discussed with management.

ADOPTED TO THE *RIGHT* HOME

The Shelter Representatives should be committed to the mandate of finding the RIGHT life long home that can meet the specific needs of each animal. This can be accomplished by having an adoption process of completing an application for adoption, having an interview, spending quality time with the animal for consideration, and completing a home check. Although a follow up is just as important as the above steps, it is not always feasible. Adopters are requested to send in a written update and photos for the adoption binder or brag board. All information received is added to the animal's file for safe record-keeping.

Another way to be highly successful is to have an adoption binder full of general and pre-approved applications for adoption. It is a matter of simply contacting the applicant, having them meet the available animal and determining if it is the RIGHT match. Experience and experimenting with this concept has proven to be highly successful.

❝ My love, a love that's
through and through.
For my loyal friend, **❞**
my dog, that's you.

~ **Anonymous**

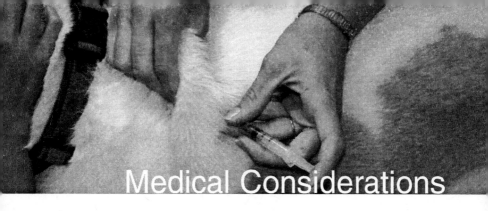

Medical Considerations

Animal Welfare Representatives and Officers may seek medical treatment for any animal found in need of a veterinarian's care, to a maximum of the amount set by management. When treating an animal, remember to search for some form of identification to help to locate and notify its owner. The officer is responsible for implementing methods of cost recovery as determined by management.

ASSESSMENT OF PHYSICAL AND VITAL CONDITIONS

The following outline is intended as an aid in the evaluation of dogs that are brought into your shelter. The outline was developed by Dr. Lane at Coast Mountain Veterinary Services in Whistler and Pemberton, B.C., Canada. It is meant to help the attending Officer during straightforward evaluations and is not intended as a replacement for proper veterinary care. If any doubt exists about the condition of the dog, call a veterinarian. Failure to do so could result in unpleasant confrontations should the animal's condition degenerate while in your care.

Check Identity

Please remember to check the right ear of all animals. Purebreds may have been tattooed in the groin area. If an identification tattoo exists, the owner's phone number can be traced through the local veterinary facility or local kennel club. Please also remember to scan for a microchip. The owner's information can be traced through microchip companies, such as AVID CANADA.

Attitude

Is the dog bright, alert and reactive (BAR)? Does it appear to be in pain? Dogs that appear "full of life" are not in critical condition. Dogs that hang their heads, breathe abnormally, or appear in discomfort, may be suffering from mild or severe illnesses, depending on their personalities and pain thresholds.

Respiration

Is it normal? Panting is a normal sign of anxiety. Abnormal breathing sounds or difficulty breathing should be considered an emergency.

Mucus Membranes

Lift up the upper lip (in non-aggressive dogs) to assess the color of the gums above the upper teeth. Are they brick red, light pink, faintly tinted pink, white, or blue? Assess the Capillary Refill Time; is it greater than two seconds? Dogs with gums that are not light pink, or that have a CRT>2 seconds should be considered emergencies.

To assess CRT, apply digital pressure to the gum and release. The gum should have turned white where your finger was pressing. Count the amount of time (1-steamboat, 2-steamboat, etc.) until the gum has turned pink again. Normal dogs will show a brisk CRT and refill in less than two seconds. Failure to do so indicates early shock. Failure to determine the CRT because the gums are too white indicates severe shock. Black pigmentation of the gums is normal; try to assess the non-black areas.

Hydration

Are the gums dry and tacky to the touch (mild dehydration)? When you lift the scruff over the shoulders, does the skin snap back into place, or sag slowly (severe dehydration)? Dogs with mild dehydration, that seem fine otherwise and can hold down water, can be monitored at the shelter. Other dogs should be referred to the veterinarian.

Body Condition

Is the hair coat dry and brittle? Can you see the ribs? Can you pinch a bony ridge along the shoulder blades? Can you feel points on the sides of the spine between the ribs and the pelvis? In most dogs, this could be recent or chronic weight loss. In dogs that are otherwise normal, this should be pointed out to the owner at the time of release. In dogs with other signs of illness, poor body condition underlines the severity of the condition.

Rectal Temperature

Normal dog values are 38°C-39.5°C in the summer and 37.5°C-39.0°C for dogs that stay outside in the winter. Values beyond these ranges indicate potential problems. Values above 40.0°C or below 37.0°C should be considered quite serious.

Abdomen

Is there pain on palpation of the abdomen? A distended painful abdomen should always be considered a crisis, requiring immediate medical attention, assuming that the animal is otherwise acting sick.

Cuts and Wounds

Superficial scrapes that do not fully puncture the skin should be cleaned and monitored. A veterinarian should see lacerations that penetrate the full thickness of the skin.

Eyes

Spastic blinking, rubbing or swelling of the eye should be regarded as an emergency. Unilateral or asymmetric discharges from the eye merits medical attention. Mild, bilaterally symmetrical discharges with no signs of irritation should be pointed out to the owner at the time of discharge.

Diarrhea

Dark black stools, or stools containing frank blood should receive medical attention. Diarrhea, in an otherwise normal dog, is likely due to stress/diet changes and can be treated by withholding food for 24 hours and monitoring. Diarrhea in a dog that appears otherwise sick should be regarded as an infectious hazard and medical attention should be sought.

Vomiting

Vomiting in an otherwise healthy dog should be monitored. Vomiting that prevents the ingestion of water for 18 hours, food for 24 hours, or in a dog that is in distress, merits a veterinary consultation. Blood in the vomit should be regarded as an emergency.[6]

SICK OR INJURED ANIMALS

This matter is considered urgent. If a complaint is received regarding an injured animal, one must respond promptly to the call. In the case of a life-threatening emergency an animal will most likely be medically treated and stay at the veterinarian clinic until it is claimed by the owner.

Any animal that is either found, or turned in to an Animal Shelter that is sick or injured shall be taken to a veterinarian for medical attention. A manager must approve medical treatments beyond a basic examination and stabilization.

DECEASED ANIMALS

When an Animal Shelter receives a call regarding a dead animal on a road or public place, the Animal Welfare Officer is dispatched to pick up the animal. The Animal Welfare Officer should take every measure available to notify the owner. If an owner is not found, the animal should be taken to a veterinarian clinic for disposal purposes. A description of the animal and relevant information must be recorded.

COMMON INFECTIOUS DISEASES

Proper diagnosis is essential. Contact your local veterinarian for information related to control, prevention, and treatment of diseases.

Respiratory and Viral Diseases (Dog and Cat)

Respiratory and Viral Diseases are only contagious to other animals. Here are some examples:

Parvovirus (Dog)

An animal becomes dehydrated, has severe diarrhea, and vomiting. Parvovirus can often be fatal. The virus can remain in the environment for over 6 months. It can be brought into your home on your clothes and shoes. It is extremely resistant to most cleaners. Black and tan dogs like Rottweilers and Dobermans are more susceptible to becoming infected.

Bordetella (Kennel Cough - Dog)

Symptoms of this airborne illness include: coughing, sneezing, and wheezing. The cough is often described as a "honking" sound or a dry hacking cough.

Distemper (Dog and Cat)

An animal suffering from this extremely contagious disease will have respiratory symptoms, eye and nasal discharge, vomiting, diarrhea, and conditions of the nervous system including convulsions or uncoordinated movements. Distemper is often fatal.

Upper Respiratory Infections (Cat)

Watch for sneezing, eye and nasal discharge.

External Parasites

Fleas (Dog and Cat)

Scratching, chewing at skin, raw skin areas, and potential hair loss are all indications of a flea infestation.

Ticks (Dog and Cat)

Ticks must be visually spotted and carefully removed in their entirety. If the head of a tick is left behind, it could lead to infection.

Ear Mites (Dog and Cat)

Symptoms of a dog or cat with ear mites include: scratching ears, shaking head, tipping the head to one side, excessive buildup of dark wax and/or bad odor from the ears.

Internal Parasites

Heartworm (Dogs and Cats)

Weight loss, coughing after exertion and bloating may all indicate heartworm. This parasite is not detected unless a blood test is done. Preventative treatment is encouraged since heartworm is usually fatal.

Hookworm and Whipworm (Microscopic - Dogs and Cats)

Symptoms of hookworm and whipworm include: weight loss, poor coat condition, and diarrhea (which may be bloody). A broad-spectrum dewormer like DRONTAL is recommended.

In dogs, Drontal PLUS removes hookworm, roundworm and tapeworm.

In cats, Drontal removes hookworm, roundworm and tapeworm.

Roundworm (Dogs and Cats)

The stool contains long, flat white worms that look like spaghetti.

Tapeworm (Dogs and Cats)

Small flat white worms can sometimes be seen in the stool. "Rice-like" segments are usually seen around the anus. Long segmented strands can be seen if vomited.

Coccidia (Dogs and Cats)

Look for weight loss, poor coat condition, and diarrhea (may be bloody), bloody stool, and abdominal discomfort.

ZOONOTIC DISEASES

Zoonotic Diseases spread from animals to people and other animals.

Rabies

Rabies can be transmitted to humans or other animals by coming into contact with the saliva (i.e., bites) or an open wound of an infected animal. An infected animal displays unusual changes in its behaviour, i.e., is very lethargic, staggers, and is abnormally aggressive. The brain of the deceased animal needs to be sent for testing to detect rabies.

Sarcoptic Mange

An infestation of mites can cause extreme itching followed by flaky or scabby dandruff and loss of hair.

Leptospiroses

This infection comes from forms of contact with the contaminated urine of infected animals, usually from contaminated surface water, as the organism can survive there for extended periods. Symptoms displayed by animals include: fever, diarrhea, vomiting and jaundice.

Ringworm

This infection is caused by a fungus cultured from the coats of dogs and cats. The carrier can pass ringworm on without showing any symptoms. Displayed symptoms can be itchiness, scratching, hair loss, and lesions that do not always form a ring. If the fungus is on the foot, then it is called *athlete's foot*. If the fungus is on the body rather than the foot, it is called *ringworm*. Ringworm is very contagious and can be spread to the human mouth and genitalia.

BYLAWS

Animal Welfare Officers are required to investigate occurrences and seek compliance through public education, encouraging responsible pet ownership, and enforcement of municipal bylaw regulations.

It is necessary for all Animal Welfare Officers to understand municipal bylaws and provincial statutory regulations and be able to prove elements of an offense should prosecution proceedings be necessary.

STATUTORY RESTRICTIONS ON ANIMAL WELFARE OFFICERS

Provincial statutes such as the "Prevention of Cruelty to Animals Act", the "Livestock Protection Act" and the "Criminal Code" are restricted to enforcement by either an "Agent" appointed by the Society for the Prevention of Cruelty to Animals or a "Peace Officer" as defined under provincial statutory regulations.

Municipalities shall provide their Animal Welfare Officers with direction as to when they should become involved or assist other agencies. The only provincial statute Animal Welfare Officers have authority to enforce with respect to dangerous dogs is the "Community Charter Act."

VICIOUS AND DANGEROUS DOGS

These matters are considered urgent and an Animal Welfare Officer must respond promptly to a call. It is recommended that all Animal Welfare Officers be provided with regular training sessions in keeping with officer safety practices and equipment. In addition, a vicious dog binder should be implemented to identify animals which could pose a risk to the public, other animals, and Animal Welfare Officers.

Vicious dogs: Animal Welfare Officers should refer to their municipal bylaw authority in handling less serious matters involving dogs that have the potential to cause harm or that have caused harm to people or domestic animals.

Dangerous dogs: Animal Welfare Officers have been given additional authority under the "Community Charter Act" and should refer to it in handling more serious cases. The Animal Welfare Officer determines if a dog is dangerous (see *dangerous dog* definition under this act). The Animal Welfare Officer should assess each occurrence on an individual basis, discuss the matter with a superior, and direct any legal questions to their municipal lawyer.

AUTHORITY TO IMPOUND A DANGEROUS DOG

An Animal Welfare Officer may seize, impound, and detain a dangerous dog under the following circumstances:

Consent: Owner/occupier consents, and the AWO is allowed to enter private property to seize, impound, and detain a dog. This does not include a dwelling place.

Offense: If there is a contravention of the municipal bylaw regulation, e.g. dog at large or unlicensed.

The "Community Charter Act", which must be referred to in its full legal context, applies to all municipalities that have animal control services and municipal bylaws concerning animal welfare. Regional districts without animal control services by bylaw can exercise authority under the "Livestock Protection Act" to apply for provincial court orders for the destruction of dangerous dogs. The "Community Charter" allows for the following:

Warrant: An Animal Welfare Officer can present evidence before a Justice of the Peace for a warrant to seize, impound, and detain a dangerous dog. If a warrant is issued, the Animal Welfare Officer with a Peace Officer shall attend to "the place" on the date and time frame specified on the warrant to search and seize the dangerous dog described and named in the warrant. The warrant authorizes the Animal Welfare Officer and Peace Officer to enter and search property including a dwelling place (refer to the Criminal Code for the legal definition of a dwelling place) to execute the warrant.

Imminent Danger: If there is imminent danger to the public and it is not feasible for the Animal Welfare Officer to obtain a warrant, they can, accompanied by a Peace Officer, enter into private property, other than a dwelling place, to seize, impound, and detain a dangerous dog.

PROVINCIAL COURT ORDER FOR DESTRUCTION

- An Animal Welfare Officer can apply for a provincial court order for the destruction of a dangerous dog. This process can be started before or after a dog is in custody. If a matter is serious, the Animal Welfare Officer should lawfully seize the dog if its whereabouts are known. Otherwise, get a court order and then obtain a warrant to seize.

- Once a dangerous dog is under the custody of a shelter, an application for destruction must be before the court within 21 days (contact your municipal lawyer to start the process) for the impoundment to continue, or the dog shall be returned to its rightful owner.

- If an application for a provincial court order for destruction is initiated, the matter is before the court and the dog can be held at a shelter until a decision is made about the dog(s).

- It is important for the Animal Welfare Officer to remember that the matter is under investigation until the case is finalized.

OBTAIN A WARRANT

To obtain a warrant in person, the following steps should be taken:

- The Animal Welfare Officer completes the "Information to Obtain a Search Warrant" and the "Warrant to Search and Seize" forms and attends the appropriate court location to request a meeting with a Justice of the Peace. The Animal Welfare Officer should be prepared to provide additional information, other than the forms, should it be requested by the justice.

- If the Animal Welfare Officer is given a (signed) warrant, then arrangements shall be made for it to be executed. Once executed, an Animal Welfare Officer then submits the "Report to a Justice" form at the appropriate court location.[7]

Vicious and Dangerous Dogs

There are many forms of aggression, which may stem from a dog's perception that it needs to defend itself by using its mouth. The investigating officer should try to determine why the dog bit as there is always a reason behind every bite. The motivation to bite may be directly related to a medical condition, which the dog is sensitive to. It therefore may bite as a way of protecting itself. On the other hand, a dog may be behaviorally unhealthy. There are also several other factors to consider: genetics, socialization, breed function, nutrition, health, learned "owner-influenced" behavior, or lack of proper training.

Early on in an investigation, the owner should be notified of a biting incident and that they should keep their dog properly contained while the matter is under investigation. After an incident is investigated, the Animal Welfare Officer will advise the owner accordingly. Verbal and written material should be issued to the owner (i.e., copy of the bylaw, ticket, recommendation of a Certified Trainer/Behavior Counselor, and information about where to purchase a muzzle), followed up by a letter confirming the dog has been declared as "vicious" under the bylaw. The situation may still need to be monitored and followed up on a regular basis. It is recommended that a vicious dog ledger be implemented.

There are a few things to keep in mind when conducting an investigation:

What were the circumstances surrounding the incident? Did the dog that barks at the mail carrier, get out and bite?

Try to assess the level of provocation - Is the dog uncomfortable around certain people or things?

Bite - Are there sustained injuries to a person or another animal? Did the dog tear clothing? Do you have medical records of injuries?

Bite potential - What is the degree of the injuries?

Breed - What was the dog bred for?

More than one dog - Which dog caused the injury?

Temperament - Does the dog have a good temperament or is it likely to show a form of aggression?

History - Generally, a dog that has bitten is likely to bite again and the degree of injuries will likely increase with each incident. Are there any reports of forms of aggression displayed by this dog?

Does the owner have a desire to change and help their dog by setting up a good safety management plan? Do you feel the owner is going to follow bylaw regulations?

AGGRESSIVE BEHAVIOR

The following types of aggression are most commonly seen in dogs, but can be displayed by other animals such as an injured cat. The Animal Welfare Officer is not responsible for informing a pet owner of a dog's specific form of aggression. That should be left up to a Certified Trainer/Behavior Counselor.

Aggressive behavior is described in two categories: offensive aggression and defensive aggression.

Offensive Aggression

Offensive types of aggression seen by dogs include protective-territorial, dominance, and predatory aggression.

Protective-Territorial Aggression

A protective-territorial dog can be protective of its home, yard and in some cases neighboring property or neighborhood. This also includes protective behavior of its owner, family members (pack members), or owner's car, when the dog perceives a threat, even if there is no real threat. For example: Animal Welfare Officers often follow up reports of dogs biting mail carriers. Often this dog is described as "going ballistic" when the mail carrier is in the vicinity of its home. From the dog's perspective it thinks it has driven the mail carrier (the threat) away after the mail has been delivered.

Dominance Aggression

The dominant dog shows aggression when it is defending its position after a subordinate party fails to comply with its expectations.

Predatory Aggression

Predatory aggression occurs when a dog is visually tracking, stalking, chasing and/or capturing a prey to obtain food. This type of behavior is not commonly displayed towards people.

Defensive Aggression

A defensive dog is trying to avoid an approaching person, such as an Animal Welfare Officer or another animal, or communicate that they should move away. Defensive types of aggression are generally less serious. They include fear, pain/medical, and possessive aggression.

Fear Aggression

A fear biter may bite a person if approached or touched unexpectedly, too quickly, or cornered. A fear biter is often described as attacking from behind and then moving away. This is different from a behaviorally healthy dog that does not display an aggressive response (growling, biting, etc.), if afraid.

Pain/Medical Aggression

Pain aggression can be displayed by a dog who is reacting to being hit. It may have a medical condition or it has been injured, etc. If a dog is injured and can't stand on its own, the Animal Welfare Officer should approach cautiously from the side and muzzle (unless the dog is unconscious), before assisting and transporting.

Possessive Aggression

A possessive dog guards food or objects. This dog may give a warning to stay away from its object and failure to do so may result in a threat or a bite. A bite can vary depending on the dog and the guarded object, e.g., raw bone. Dogs that are more assertive in their aggression can inflict serious injury such as multiple bites.

Other Forms of Aggression

Other types of aggression that can be displayed are: dog-to-dog, redirected, and mixed aggression.

Dog to Dog Aggression

Dog-to-dog aggression can be fear based, dominance, pack (changes with status), or gender specific. Every shelter should test to see if they have a dog that is dog aggressive in general or is gender specific. This is very important before the dog goes out with a volunteer dog walker and/or is placed in an exercise area to socialize with other dogs.

Redirected Aggression

Redirected aggression can occur when a dog is showing aggression to a person or other animal going by its property and the aggression is blocked by something such as a fence. The dog will then redirect its aggression towards another person or other animal in close proximity, such as another dog in the yard. Animal Welfare Officers have to be mindful of this when bringing a new dog into a kennel area as they could be subject to redirected aggression.

Mixed Aggression

Mixed aggression is a combination of defensive and offensive aggression. A fearful dog can also be protective and territorial of its home. Furthermore, a fearful dog may be more assertive in the presence of a pack of dogs.

In conclusion, owners have a duty to set their companion up for success and to provide a safe environment. If a dog is displaying forms of aggression, the owner should take preventative measures to ensure public safety. They should be referred to a Certified Trainer/Behavior Counselor.

BITES

A bite is a sign of aggression and force. Dogs that are biting and causing injury should be muzzled. Any contact which leaves some sort of injury can be categorized as a form of aggression. Most bites are inhibited and do not result in serious injury, meaning that the dog made a choice not to bite more seriously.

Example: A dog could give a threat - snap and miss, use its mouth without leaving a visible mark, use its mouth with minimum pressure leaving a red mark or bruise, or a canine puncture. A dog may give a full bite causing significant injury or multiple bites, causing serious injury or death.[8]

BITING INCIDENTS

There are numerous factors, which must be considered when dealing with biting incidents, but the call MUST be responded to immediately. Public safety and the identification of the dog and/or dogs is paramount. Another factor to consider is the degree of injuries received by either the person or other animal. In many cases, it may be in the public's best interest to have the dog seized and impounded. The investigating Animal Welfare Officer should try to determine:

- Who is the complainant, witness, and victim?
- Who is prepared to attend court?
- Who was interviewed?
- Who still needs to be interviewed?
- Who is the dog?
- Who is the subject dog owner?
- Who was in charge of the dog(s) at the time of the incident?
- What happened? Was the bite provoked or unprovoked?
- What type of offense was committed?
- What was the degree of injury?
- What clinic, hospital, doctor attended to the victim?
- What did the dog owner say?
- What responses were taken by the alleged dog owner?
- What information was documented? i.e., pictures, diagrams, doctor's report, and statements.
- What action did you take? What action do you still need to take?
- What other agencies assisted?
- What is your authority? Should the dog be declared as a vicious dog (send out a bite letter) or do you have reasonable and probable grounds to believe this dog is dangerous? Is it in the public's interest to have the dog seized?
- Where is the dog? Is there still a threat to public safety?
- Where was the location of the incident?
- Where was the dog at the time of the incident?
- Where was the dog owner at the time of the incident?
- When did this happen?
- When was it was reported?

- When did you receive a report of the incident?
- When did you arrive on scene?
- When did you speak to anyone?
- When did other help arrive to assist?
- Why did this happen?

INTERVIEWING THE VICTIM

When interviewing victims it is important to understand that they may not only have physical injuries, but emotional injuries as well. One example of emotional injury may be that they are no longer comfortable going outside in their yard and going for walks in their neighborhood out of a real fear of dogs. Victims may feel depressed, anxious, nervous, or fearful, and may be suffering from Post Traumatic Stress Disorder. The investigating Animal Welfare Officer seeing or hearing such symptoms should refer victims to Mental Health Practitioners or Family Physicians.

VISIT TO THE DOCTOR

If a victim is at a hospital, you may wish to ask the attending physician if the injuries can be documented before they are bandaged. This is not always convenient, so at the very least you may be able to get a verbal description from the physician, or when interviewing the victim. At times, it may warrant consent of the report being released for your records.

❝If there are
no dogs in Heaven,
then **when I die**
I want to go
where they went.❞

~ **Anonymous**

ANIMAL WELFARE OFFICER EQUIPMENT

It is important to check your duty vehicle and all of your equipment to ensure it is in good functioning order. Animal handling in the field can be demanding and at times crucial. It is essential to have humane equipment and take control of situations for animal and public safety.

Communication

Radios, base station, and phones.

Duty Bag Equipment List

- Business cards
- Extra notebook, two pens, a pencil, and extra paper for diagrams
- "Mini Mag" for the duty belt and/or a regular size flashlight
- Camera to photograph dogs that are routinely at-large, bites, or cruelty matters
- Measuring tape to measure bites, etc.
- Fan folder for important contact numbers, forms, and extra copies of bylaws
- Binder containing all animal bylaws, statutes, and reference material
- Ticket book holder with warning notices and tickets
- Traffic safety vest with reflective strips or lettering "AWO"
- Extra licenses
- Bait, leashes, and muzzles
- Map
- Sunglasses
- Water
- The Animal Care Reference Guide

Gloves

Thick gloves or "Kevlar" gloves will give you some protection against bites and scratches, but can change the "feeling" when you're handling an animal. This could mean you are not using enough pressure to properly restrain an animal, or too much, which can hurt an animal. Keep a supply of disposable gloves available for handling animals that may have contagious diseases, or may be injured and/or are dead.

Rope, Leashes

The leash should be six feet long with a loop at one end that can be slipped around the animal's head without your hands getting too close to its face. If the leash is clipped onto a dog's collar, it should also be looped around a dog's neck to prevent it from escaping.

Snappy Snare

A "Snappy Snare" is used when it is not possible to get close enough to an animal to use a leash. It allows you to approach and slip a loop over a fast moving or "standoffish" dog. It can also be used on the head of an injured animal that needs assistance.

Bite Stick

If a dog is going to bite, it will bite whatever is out in front of it. A bite (deterrent) stick can be used in a semi circle out in front of you to keep a dog at a distance. It also also allows the dog to direct its bite on to something other than you. If you don't carry a bite stick, a ticket book or some other object may be useful to direct the dog's bite away from you. It is recommended that Animal Welfare Officers look into training that certifies the use of a bite stick if used to "drop" an attacking dog. You may be called to justify your use of force.

Snare Pole

When you approach a dog with a snare pole, open the loop and hold it below the dog's head allowing it to sniff the pole. Slip the loop over the dog's head and tighten it just enough to prevent escape. The dog can then be directed into your vehicle or shelter. For cats, the loop can be slipped over their heads and then behind their front legs.

Cat Tongs

Cat tongs allow you to restrain uncooperative or vicious cats, humanely and safely. Place the tongs around the cat's neck and make sure you have a transport cage ready.

Transport Cages

Transport cages provide a temporary, safe area for animals and protection for the animal care giver.

Rescue Bag

Towels, blankets, and pillowcases work well for the capture of small animals. Rope leashes, regular leashes, muzzles (different sized), soft food with pull back lids, (or canned foods with a can opener), identification tags, disposable bags, disposable gloves, and a throw net are all items that should be stored in a rescue bag.

To improvise a muzzle, hold onto a piece of rope behind the dog's ear and lead the other end down the side of its neck and under the chin. Wrap the muzzle around the dog's snout a couple of times and then tie the ends together behind its ears.

Back Board

A Back Board is used to assist the injured and to remove deceased animals. Back Boards can be made out of a sheet of wood with handles on both sides for lifting. There are a variety of styles available through animal control equipment suppliers.

Nets

Nets can be used for small, hard-to-catch, moving, or injured animals. There are a variety of sizes and styles on the market to consider. Make sure to remove an animal and transfer it into a transport cage or safe area after being caught. Inspect the net after each use.

Collapsible Humane Traps

Humane traps are at times necessary and should be on hand if needed. At minimum, three different sizes should be ordered. If you set up a trap in a shaded area, it should be checked every 2 hrs. - 12 hrs. maximum to make sure the animal is protected from the weather, and that there are not any extended periods without any food, water, shelter, and care. Attach a sign to the trap explaining its purpose and request that the shelter be contacted if an animal is inside the trap.

Duty Vehicle

Mini-vans and pick-up trucks are most commonly used as Duty Vehicles. Additional features and equipment should include:

- Flashing yellow lights on the front and back grill for officer safety
- A hand-held spot light for identifying injured animals and locating civic addresses when responding in an after-hours emergency
- Stainless steel sloped cages for ease of sanitization

- An adjustable divider to separate animals if needed or to open up for the transport of an injured animal on a stretcher
- Easily sanitized rubberized matting to prevent animals from slipping
- A storage area between the seats for storage of routinely used equipment
- A storage area for a stretcher, snare pole, cat tongs, throw net, rescue equipment bag, additional transport cages, and a collapsible shovel
- A safety door for viewing vicious or dangerous animals during unloading
- Window screens to prevent the escape of an animal
- A computer, which can be effective for time management and officer safety.

" He is your **friend,**
your **partner,** your **defender,**
and your dog.
You are his **life,** his **love,**
and his leader.
He will be yours, faithful and true,
to the last beat of his heart.
You owe it to him to be **"**
worthy of such devotion.

~ **Anonymous**

Disaster Preparedness for Companions

It is essential that everyone and their communities be prepared should a natural or man made disaster strike. Supplies for all family members and companion animals for a minimum of a week should be on hand.

GETTING READY

The following is a list of supplies that are required for your animal in case of disaster.

Food and Water

- Have at least a one week's supply at all times
- If pets eat canned food, buy pop-top cans of food small enough to be used at one feeding
- Store food in an airtight, waterproof container
- A food dish, spoon, and a manual can opener
- Drinking water for at least a week for each animal
- An extra dish in case one is lost
- Try to maintain a regular feeding schedule
- Chew toys

Harness or Breakaway Collar with Tag

- Harness and identification tag
- Extra collar with spare identification tag that can be written on in case one is lost or for temporary relocation
- 6-foot leash for walks
- Chain (cannot be chewed through) that can be attached to a metal stake

Confining

- A plastic or wire collapsible crate to transport the pet should evacuation become necessary, and for temporary confinement. Include favorite pet toy.
- A metal stake that screws into the ground, with a place to fasten a chain
- Leash to keep your dog safely controlled during walks

First Aid Kit

- Absorbent gauze pads
- Absorbent gauze roll
- Antiseptic wipes or pump spray
- Bandage
- Blankets
- Conforming bandages
- Cotton tipped applicators
- Disposable gloves
- First aid book for dogs/cats/other
- Instant cold pack
- Magazine (splint)
- Muzzle fitted for your pet
- Adhesive tape
- Rescue remedy
- Tweezers and scissors
- Towels
- Vet wrap
- Waterproof bag

Medications

- Minimum of a week's supply of medication, if applicable. Back up supply for pets on long term medication.

Sanitation

- Waste bags/litter box and scoop
- Supply of litter for a least a week
- Supply of plastic bags for disposal

Cleaning

- A small container of soap for cleaning
- Paper towels for drying dishes and clean up
- If housing a pet in a crate, include a disinfectant for cleaning the crate

Other hints

- If you are going on vacation and leaving your pet with someone else, be sure to have discussed with them a plan to take care of your animal in the event of a disaster.

- If you're kenneling your dog or cat, does the facility have a plan in place should a disaster occur? Check with your veterinarian.

- Rotate food at least once every three months.

- If tap water is not suitable for humans to drink, it is not suitable for pets to drink either.

- Store water in a cool, dark place, and rotate it once every two months.

- Microchip and/or tattoo animals so they have forms of permanent identification.

- Have copies of your animal's medical records, including records of its vaccination history.

- When restraining your dog, use a chain, attached to a harness, and make sure your dog is tethered away from hazards.

- Cats will probably find a safe place within their normal territory to hide. Place food out close to the location where they can eat.

- Have some pictures of your animal in case they get lost. If is also good to include yourself in some of the pictures in case you have to prove ownership. Store pictures in resealable plastic bag.

RESCUERS EQUIPMENT LIST

- Address/phone book
- Bucket of oats (or shake stones in bucket)
- Cell phone with vehicle charger or regular charger
- Change of clothes
- Collapsible cages
- Compass
- Critter bags, sack bags, pillow cases
- Duct tape
- Fire extinguisher
- Food that is high-energy. Animal food for feeding that can also be used for bait.
- Garbage bags, body bags and identification tags
- Gloves for working, bite gloves and disposable
- Halters (preferably leather as nylon melts)
- Hammer and nails
- Identification
- Waterproof jacket and pants
- Leatherman
- Map of area
- Medication (yours)

- Mini Mag or regular flashlight
- Net or blankets
- Two notebooks
- Paper, forms
- Polaroid with lots of film
- Rope (leads, leashes, temporary muzzles)
- Rubber boots
- Sleeping bag/pillow
- Spray paint bottles for a marking area, where animal has been rescued
- Toilet and paper towel
- Transport vehicle
- Twine (to tie pants cuffs for working in bush)
- Vest with lots of pockets, i.e. with reflective "AWO"
- Water bottle for self and water for animals
- Waterproof pens (2-3)
- Whistle (Officer Safety)
- Wire cutters (wear on belt or duty belt)
- Zip lock bags to store supplies

ENCOURAGING STORIES ABOUT SHELTER ANIMALS

"Larry Bear" was a 12-year-old German Shepherd guard dog that lived at a business until he was later surrendered by his owner. After much time under the shelter's care and with his beloved handler, he found a very special home. He was cherished every day by his new owner and experienced a few last tender and loving years, until he sadly passed.

"Sugar" is a young female cat that was found in the early morning, reported as having been hit by a car. The responding Animal Welfare Officer determined she had not been struck by a car, but was found in grave condition due to neglect. She was rushed to a 24-hour emergency hospital and was diagnosed as critical. To the credit of her veterinarian and caregivers, "Sugar" made it through the night. She was transferred to another veterinarian hospital for two intense weeks of additional care. The staff named her "Sugar" because she was so sweet! When she was healthy enough, she was released to the shelter, and later was adopted to a new home.

"Rick" was a nine-year-old German Short-Haired Pointer who had worked all his life as a hunter's working companion. When his owner replaced him with a puppy, a friend of the owner's who didn't want to see Rick euthanized, brought Rick into the shelter. Lucky for Rick, his new prospective owner thought he was beautiful and deserved a second chance for a loving home. He was vaccinated and neutered, and four growths were removed from his head, ear canal, chest and paw area before he joined a new family.

Treat me kindly, my beloved friend, for no heart in all the world is more grateful for kindness than the loving heart of me.

Do not break my spirit with a stick, for though I should lick your hand between blows, your patience and understanding will more quickly teach me the things you would have me learn.

Speak to me often, for your voice is the world's sweetest music, as you must know by the fierce wagging of my tail when your footstep falls upon my waiting ear.

Please take me inside when it is cold and wet, for I am a domesticated animal, no longer accustomed to bitter elements. I ask no greater glory than the privilege of sitting at your feet beside the hearth. Keep my pan filled with fresh water, for I cannot tell you when I suffer thirst.

Feed me clean food that I may stay well, to romp and play and do your bidding, to walk by your side and stand ready, willing and able to protect you with my life, should your life be in danger.

And, my friend, when I am very old, and I no longer enjoy good health, hearing and sight, do not make heroic efforts to keep me going. I am not having any fun. Please see that my trusting life is taken gently. I shall leave this earth knowing with the last breath I draw that my fate was always safest in your hands.

~Author unknown

[1] Cpl. Gil Puder, Vancouver Police Department. *Use of Force Training Manual for Bylaw Enforcement Officers,* Rev. (1994).

Siddle, Bruce K. and White, Wally. *PPCT Defensive Tactics Instructors Manual,* 2nd Rev. (1991), PPCT Management System, Inc., Millstadt, Illinois (1989).

[2] Vancouver Police Department. *Municipal Bylaw Enforcement – Note Taking and Notebook Format,* student handout.

Police Academy, Justice Institute of British Columbia. *Developing Investigative Skills - Note Taking and Maintaining Notebooks,* student handout.

Royal Canadian Mounted Police. *Evidence Collection,* Auxiliary notes.

[3] Law Enforcement Training Institute, University of Missouri – Columbia. *Field Note Taking,* student handout and notes.

[4] Royal Canadian Mounted Police, Canada. *File Presentation,* Auxiliary handout.

[5] Hetts, Susan, PhD and Estep, Daniel, PhD. *ACT – Animal Care Training in collaboration with the Humane Society of the United States, Canine Behavior - Body Postures and Evaluating Behavioral Health* (2000).

[6] Dr. Lane, Coast Mountain Veterinary Services, Whistler and Pemberton, British Columbia, provided the *Assessment of Physical and Vital Conditions,* handout.

[7] Queens Printer, Victoria, British Columbia. *Community Charter (SBC 2003), Chapter 26.* Available: www.qp.gov.bc.ca/statreg

[8] Smith, Cheryl Margaret, Kemptville, Ontario. *Biting, Barking, Lunging, Growling, Retraining Your Dog without Intimidation.*

Cpl. Gil Puder, Vancouver Police Department, British Columbia. *Outline for Human Relations Training for Whistler Enforcement Officers,* student handout, Rev. (1992).

Police Academy, Justice Institute of British Columbia. *Introduction to Cruelty to Animal Investigations,* student manual and handouts (2001).

Vancouver Police Department, British Columbia. *Court Procedures,* student worksheet.

Halligan, Joanne, Instructor, *Society for the Prevention of Cruelty to Animals – Pet First Aid, Petcetra Practical First Aid for Animals Manual,* Rev. (1996).

Law Enforcement Training Institute, University of Missouri Columbia. *Restraints,* student handout (1998).

Royal Canadian Mounted Police. *Officer Survival is based on "Preparation" not "Paranoia",* Auxiliary handout.

Highlands Animal Hospital and Seymour Animal Care Clinic, North Vancouver, British Columbia. *Worms: A Guide for Prevention and Control,* handout.

United Nations – Emergency Animal Rescue, Justice Institute of British Columbia. *Keeping Your Own Companion Animal Safe during a Disaster and Rescuers Equipment,* student manual.

Wikipedia, Encyclopedia, Wikipedia.org. *Transferable Diseases* (2006).

James M.Griffin, MD, and Lisa D. Carlson, DVM. *Dog owner's Home Veterinary Handbook,* 3rd edition (2000).

Polsky, Richard H, PhD., CAAB - Certified Applied Animal Behaviorist, President, Animal Behavior Counseling Services, Inc., Los Angeles, California. *Issues about Animal Behavior Relevant to Dog-bite Statutes,* Rev. (2005).

Marder, Amy, DVM, Rodle Press, Inc. *Your Healthy Pet – Your Dog's Vaccinations* (1994).

Ciba Animal Health, Century Avenue, Mississauga, Ontario, Ltd. *Parasites & Dogs: What every dog owner should know.*

Howard, Tom. *Hamlyn All Colour Guide to Cats.* Reed International Books Limited (1993).

Smith, Cheryl Margaret. *Biting, Barking, Lunging, Growling - Retraining Your Dog Without Intimidation.*

Crisp, Terry and Glen, Samantha. *Out of Harm's Way - The Extraordinary True Story of One Women's Devotion to Animal Rescue.*

Kehret, Peg. *Shelter Dogs - Amazing Stories of Adopted Strays.*

Peachey, Erica. *Understanding your DOG - An illustrated guide to understanding your dog's behavior.*

Abrantes, Rodger. *Dog Language.*

Kilcommons, Brian and Wilson, Sarah. *PAWS TO CONSIDER - Choosing the right dog for you and your family.*

Christiansen, Bob. *Save Our Strays - How We Can End Pet Overpopulation and Stop Killing Healthy Cats and Dogs.*

Video Tape Programs and Workbooks

ACT – "Animal Shelter Training Program"
Six video tape programs and workbooks: *People Care/Kennel Care, Animal Handling & Safety, Animal Identification, Dog and Cat basics, Vaccinations and Preventative Health, Fleas, Ticks and other Parasites.*
Available at: **www.4act.com**

Kimberly Lord has loved and cared for animals since she came nose to nose with her family's first dog, "Buddy". Her desire to help animals led her to pursue a 15-year career as a Bylaw, Animal Welfare Officer and to national certification as an Animal Care Professional. She was only the 3rd person in Canada to receive this designation.

Kimberly has overseen the Animal Welfare Service for the Resort Municipality of Whistler, the Village of Pemberton, and the District of North Vancouver, British Columbia, Canada. As the Coordinator of the Volunteer Animal Disaster Preparedness Team for Whistler, she organized enough emergency supplies to help up to 500 animals in the event of an emergency. Her extensive training, both in Canada and the United States, includes multiple certificates related to bylaw enforcement, animal welfare, cruelty investigation, animal rescue, and first aid care. She also served as an RCMP Auxiliary Constable for six years in Whistler.

About Animal Welfare Consulting Inc.

Animal Welfare Consulting Inc. is a business located in North Vancouver, British Columbia, Canada. It offers quality instructional training for Animal Welfare Officers and Shelter Representatives, and helps participants apply skills to serve their human and animal communities as Animal Care Professionals.
Visit: **www.animalwelfareconsulting.com**

NOTES

NOTES

NOTES

NOTES

ISBN 141209571-9